Introduc[tion]

For nearly 400 years (A.D. 43–410) Britain was a province of the Roman Empire. Throughout the Empire, from Britain to the Middle East, Roman coinage was the regular currency, and Latin was the official language. This book examines evidence, historical and archaeological, of life in Britain during the Roman occupation.

Excavations of such towns as Verulamium (St. Albans) and of such villas as Bignor in Sussex as well as finds of tools, pottery and ornaments, illustrate civilian life. Tombs of soldiers and remains of fortresses and weapons help to explain military life. Coins, commemorating achievements, and inscriptions on buildings, altars and tombs, throw light on people and events.

Evidence from other parts of the Roman Empire is used: some tombstones from *Gaul*[1] portray domestic life; the Emperor Trajan's column in Rome shows the army at work; and some Latin writers, such as *Caesar* and *Tacitus*, comment on the Roman occupation of Britain.

Even before the legions were recalled to Rome (A.D. 410) and the occupation ended, the British province was exposed to barbarian invaders. They finally wiped out much of the Roman civilisation, but some features of it later became part of the life of English people. Many Roman fortresses were abandoned or destroyed, but others, such as Portus Adurni (Portchester), were reoccupied during the *Middle Ages*. The villas were deserted, and not until the fifteenth century was it again safe for people to live in unfortified country houses; and these later houses lacked Roman heat-ing [...] were use[...] the medieval tower of St. Albans Abbey. The routes of some Roman roads, such as the one now known as Watling Street, which ran from Dubris (Dover) to Deva (Chester), are still used. The chess-board pattern of Roman Ratae (Leicester), among others, is still preserved in the modern street plan. It was during the Roman occupation London developed as a centre.

The peace of the later Empire allowed the growth of Christianity in Britain, and in certain areas it survived the barbarian invasions. Later, in 597, St. Augustine was sent by the Pope from Rome to reintroduce the Latin liturgy to the whole of Britain. In medieval *Christendom* Latin became the international language of the church, literature and learning, and it is still used all over the world in the Roman Catholic liturgy and in the scientific naming of plants and animals. Many of our everyday words also derive from Latin. During the Renaissance (fourteenth to sixteenth centuries), Greek and Roman art, architecture and literature were given a new appreciation and began to exercise a new influence.

The modern countries of Western Europe owe much to the Greek and Roman civilisation which was preserved by the 'pax Romana' (Roman peace). Roman law, which had made possible the development of Roman art and literature, later became the basis of the law of many European nations. It is therefore worth-while studying Roman Britain, in order to begin to appreciate this greater civilisation behind it.

[1] The meaning of words printed like *this* are to be found in the Glossary on page 59.

ROMAN SOLDIERS BUILDING A CAMP. Inside the turf rampart legionaries are levelling the ground. Outside it they are digging the ditch. What tools are they using? Notice the two legionaries quarrelling on the left. On the right Emperor Trajan is receiving an enemy chieftain, and in the foreground a *ballista* is being transported by mule.

THE ROMAN CONQUEST OF BRITAIN

In 55 B.C. *Julius Caesar* had completed his conquest of *Gaul*. He then prepared to cross the Channel and invade Britain. Although merchants had traded there for some time, most of the island was almost completely unknown. Caesar describes in his memoirs how he twice landed in Britain, defeated the British chariot-warriors and actually reached the Thames, but was forced to withdraw to deal with rebellions in Gaul.

So Britain remained outside the Imperial frontiers until A.D. 43, when Roman forces were sent by the Emperor Claudius (see page 6). They landed at the harbour of Rutupiae (Richborough) in Kent, and defeated the soldiers of Caractacus, son of Cunobelinus (Cymbeline), the most powerful British king, whose capital was Camulodunum (Colchester). The Emperor joined the army at Londinium, and marched to take Camulodunum, where the old wooden town was rebuilt in stone and set up as the first *colonia* in Britain. He formally acknowledged the island as a Roman province, and appointed a governor to preserve law and order. During the next few years Roman armies extended the boundaries, and built roads and forts as far as Mona (the Isle of Anglesey), where they defeated the *Druids*.

In A.D. 61, while they were thus occupied, Boudicca, queen of the Iceni, whose capital was at Venta (Caistor-by-Norwich), raised a British rebellion. Her warriors stormed west to sack and burn Camulodunum, Verulamium (St. Albans), and Londinium. They were defeated only after they had slaughtered several thousand Romans and pro-Roman Britons.

Still the Roman conquest continued. The writer *Tacitus* describes how his father-in-law, Agricola, advanced into northern England and Scotland (A.D. 79), and secured control of lowland Scotland by defeating the Picts at the battle of Mons Graupius (page 14). Remains still exist of the line of forts built by Agricola north of the Firth-Clyde estuaries, but he never had time to subdue the whole of Scotland.

The Roman frontier was bounded in the reign of Hadrian (page 8) by the famous Wall (page 21) built by legionaries and stretching from Tyne to Solway. It was 73 miles long, 20 feet high, and 8-10 feet wide. Along the south side of it ran a military road. In the year 140 the Emperor Antoninus Pius extended the frontier northwards by building a second wall from Firth to Clyde. This Wall was difficult to defend against sea attacks and in 185 it was abandoned.

In 192 Clodius Albinus, then governor of Britain, set out with a large army of the British garrison troops to march against Rome, but was defeated by the Emperor Septimius Severus (page 9) in Gaul. During the absence of governor and army, barbarians had poured south over Hadrian's Wall, looting and destroying as far as the legionary fortress of Eboracum (York). The Emperor Severus and his sons, Caracalla and Geta (page 11), defeated the rest of the rebels and drove back the barbarians. There remained the task of repairing the damaged fortresses and Hadrian's Wall, and when Severus died in 211 at Eboracum the work was still not complete.

By the end of the third century the province of Britain was poorer. The theatre at Verulamium (page 35) had been closed, and some stones used elsewhere. Finding Roman defences weaker, pirates from Germany and Frisia increased their raids on the British coast. The Romans strengthened defences by building a series of shore-forts (pages 21, 22). In 287 Carausius (page 11), commander of the Roman anti-pirate fleet in the Channel, was accused of co-operating with the pirates. He assembled the troops, and with their support declared himself Emperor in Britain. Only nine years later (296) did the Emperor Constantius Chlorus restore the province to Roman rule (page 12), and begin to repair the damage done to Hadrian's Wall while the troops had been called away by the usurper Carausius.

In 367 the barbarians invaded again from the North and from overseas. Finally, the Emperor Theodosius drove them back and restored the Wall. Once more, in 383, Britain was drained of Roman troops when the British governor, Magnus Maximus, rebelled against the Emperor Gratian; henceforth Hadrian's Wall was abandoned for good. When barbarians from the north of Europe invaded Italy and threatened Rome itself, the Emperor Honorius, in 410, issued a decree recalling the legions from Britain to protect the more vital centres of the Empire.

IRON AGE COIN. *Obverse or head* Can you read the name of Tascio (vanus)? He was the British king of Camulodunum (Colchester) and father of king Cunobelinus (see page 3).
Reverse or tail This British warrior was like some of those who opposed Julius Caesar.

COIN OF JULIUS CAESAR. *Obverse* The inscription reads: 'To the eternal (perpetuo) Caesar'. *Reverse* The symbols of Roman power and authority. Note the winged herald's staff which the messenger god Mercury carried; the *fasces*; the celestial globe and the axe. What else can you see?

COIN OF THE EMPEROR CLAUDIUS. *Obverse* What is he wearing? *Reverse* Simple triumphal arch (compare page 10), on which stands a horseman between two *trophies*. The rider carries a spear. What does the inscription mean?

BRONZE HEAD OF EMPEROR CLAUDIUS (A.D. 41–54). He came to Britain with the army of conquest in A.D. 43. The head was found on the Suffolk coast not far from Camulodunum (Colchester), where a temple had been built in his honour.

BRONZE HEAD OF EMPEROR HADRIAN (A.D. 117–138) found in the Thames at London Bridge. He visited Britain in A.D. 122 to inspect the new defensive wall between the Tyne and the Solway. Compare his hair-style with that of Claudius and Constantine.

STONE HEAD OF EMPEROR CONSTANTINE (A.D. 306–337) found at York. He was in Britain when his father Constantius Chlorus died and was proclaimed Emperor at York. He was the first Emperor to become a Christian.

TWO COINS OF NERO found in Britain. *Above, Obverse* Nero's head. *Reverse* Cavalrymen at exercise. S.C. stands for 'Senatus Consulto'. Coins were issued by the Emperor in the name of the Senate. *Below, Obverse* Nero's head. *Reverse* Altar of peace (Ara Pacis) at Lugdunum (Lyons) in Gaul, probably to celebrate the defeat of a rebellion.

BRONZE STATUE OF THE EMPEROR NERO (A.D. 54–68). In his reign occurred the first persecution of the Christians. This statue was found in Suffolk, but the fine workmanship suggests that it was made in Italy. Look at his decorated breastplate and his elegant boots and tunic.

COIN OF TRAJAN (A.D. 98–117). *Obverse* IMP. TRAIANO. Note his imperial wreath and the fold of *toga* over his shoulder. *Reverse* Trajan's column, celebrating his victories in Dacia in Eastern Europe. It still stands in Rome (see also pages 23, 25).

COIN OF TRAJAN. *Obverse* Can you read the Emperor's name? *Reverse* The Circus Maximus, largest of the chariot-racing arenas in Rome (page 34). The inscription means: 'The Senate and people of Rome to the most excellent Prince (Optimo Principi)'. What is the meaning of s.c.? (see page 7).

COIN OF HADRIAN (A.D. 117–138). *Obverse* HADRIANUS AUG(USTUS) CO(N)S(UL) IIII. This means: 'Hadrian Augustus Consul four years'. *Reverse* Hadrian addressing his army in Syria. They are holding standards.

COIN OF HADRIAN. *Obverse* Hadrian. *Reverse* Do you recognise this figure? What is she holding? Under her right foot is a pile of stones, perhaps representing Hadrian's Wall. Compare her with our modern version on the penny.

STONE STATUE OF SEPTIMIUS SEVERUS. His exploits are described on page 4. He died at Eboracum in A.D. 211. How is this statue like, and how unlike, that of Nero on page 7?

TRIUMPHAL ARCH OF SEPTIMIUS SEVERUS IN ROME. It was set up by the Senate to celebrate the victories of the Emperor and his son over Eastern tribes, which are represented in sculpture on the arch. Note the rounded arch and fluted columns. Remains of a small triumphal arch have been found at Verulamium. The French Emperor Napoleon built a triumphal arch (1825) in Roman style to celebrate his victories, and it is now one of the landmarks of modern Paris.

COIN OF CARACALLA (A.D. 211–17) elder son of Septimius Severus. *Obverse* Caracalla's head. *Reverse* Victory setting up a *trophy*. Another Victory stands on the right and a captive crouches below.

COIN OF GETA (A.D. 211–212) brother of Caracalla and co-Emperor with him. Caracalla brutally murdered him in his mother's arms. *Obverse* Geta's head. *Reverse* Winged Victory. Can you see Geta's title VICT. BRIT., celebrating his British victories?

COIN OF CARAUSIUS, the usurper in Britain (A.D. 287–293). *Obverse* Carausius wearing the imperial wreath. *Reverse* Jupiter. This was one of the first coins produced at the London mint (M.L.) established by Carausius.

COIN OF DECENTIUS MAGNUS (351–353). *Obverse* The Emperor's head. *Reverse* The sign ☧, representing XP(ΙΣΤΟΣ), i.e. CHR (ISTOS). Christianity was now the official religion of the Empire.

MEDALLION OF CONSTANTIUS CHLORUS (A.D. 305–306). *Obverse* What is he wearing? *Reverse* Constantius on horseback is being welcomed at the gates of London (LON), after defeating the rebels of Carausius. Note the beaked ship. How is it driven? What is the Emperor wearing and carrying?

COIN OF CONSTANTINE THE GREAT (A.D. 306–337). *Obverse* He wears a nimbus (halo of light). Christ, the Virgin Mary and the saints are often represented with a nimbus. *Reverse* Four children, representing the four seasons. Which do you think is which?

THE ROMAN ARMY

Throughout the Roman Empire were stationed some twenty-five to thirty legions, most of them in permanent fortresses guarding frontier provinces like Britain. Inscriptions on soldiers' tombs (page 15) and on buildings tell us where the legions were based and what they were doing. For instance, an inscription at York states that the walls were built by the IXth legion. Another, from a milecastle on Hadrian's Wall, states that the IInd legion built this part of the defences. During the conquest the legions were needed wherever danger threatened, so the Romans built their efficient road-system for the rapid transport of troops and equipment from one place to another.

Each legion was commanded by a prefect, assisted by six officers called tribunes. It contained about 5,000 men, all Roman citizens, divided into 60 'centuries'. Each 'century' consisted, in practice, of 75–85 men, and was commanded by a centurion (page 15), and followed its own standard (page 8) into battle.

A legionary soldier who served with the colours for 20 years received on discharge money or land. As the frontiers of the Empire expanded, however, non-citizens were recruited as auxiliary soldiers, to assist the legions. They were stationed on distant frontier posts, such as the garrisons on Hadrian's Wall (page 21), often far from their homes. Look, for instance, at the tombs of the auxiliary Rufus from Thrace in the Balkans, and of the *optio* from Spain (pages 15, 16), both of whom died on active service in Britain.

Roman camps were of two types. Soldiers on the march or in the field would choose a site, surround it with a ditch and heap the earth from the ditch into a rampart. Along the top of this they planted sharpened stakes, and thus protected they camped for the night in leather tents. The permanent camp, auxiliary fort (pages 20, 21) or big legionary fortress (page 19), was defended by a larger ditch and rampart, on which was built a stone wall. At regular intervals along the wall were towers, and between the towers were mounted catapults and stone-throwers. Through the centre of the fort ran two main roads, one passing through the east and west, the other through the north and south, gates.

At Deva (Chester) part of the north wall of the legionary fortress still stands 17 feet above the original ground-level. By the cross-roads at the centre, round a large open square, are the remains of three granaries (page 20) and of the barrack-blocks (page 19), where the soldiers lived, ate, and slept. Outside the wall there was a cemetery, and also a civilian settlement, with shops, taverns, married-quarters, amphitheatre (pages 32, 33), and public baths (pages 31, 36).

The efficiency of the army was maintained by frequent drill and exercise, and severe discipline. A sentry who slept on duty might be stoned to death by his fellow-legionaries, while a defeated unit was liable to be *decimated* by its commander. Offences were punished by flogging or death or, in milder cases, by loss of pay or rations, or by extra fatigues. The soldiers' food was simple. From their corn rations they made porridge or bread; they also ate cheese and beans, and drank mead made from honey, as well as beer. Wine was imported from Gaul and meat was a luxury. From the historian *Josephus*, we learn how they ate together and how the signal for sleep, reveille, and guard-duty was given by a bugle-call.

Every engagement was carefully planned in advance, and the battle-order followed a regular system. The Roman historian *Tacitus* tells how his father-in-law Agricola commanded the Romans at the battle of Mons Graupius (A.D. 83) in the Scottish Highlands. First, the auxiliaries fired sling-bolts and arrows (page 17), and then six light-armed auxiliary contingents closed with the enemy. Next, the auxiliaries made a series of cavalry charges, and finally broke the enemy lines. The heavily equipped legionaries took no part in this battle, but Tacitus describes how in the final defeat of Queen Boudicca (A.D. 61) the legionaries advanced in tight wedge-formation, with the support of the auxiliary infantry and cavalry.

For an idea of Roman siege-operations we may read *Josephus'* account of Vespasian's long and difficult siege of Jotapata in Judaea (A.D. 67). Here the Romans built ramparts of timber, stones, and earth, behind a line of hurdles, and set up 160 catapults to launch stones, fire-brands and arrows into the city; while battering-rams were brought up against the walls under cover of a row of shields (page 25). Vespasian had had previous experience of siege-warfare in Britain, when he took the British hill-fortress of Dunum (Maiden Castle) in Dorset, powerfully defended, as excavations have shown.

TOMBSTONE OF A CENTURION FROM COLCHESTER. This was put up by his *freedmen*. The inscription says that he was Marcus Favonius Facilis of the XX (20th) legion. In his hand he holds his staff of office. Notice his moulded body-armour, the greaves on his legs, his pleated skirt and his cloak. What weapons does he carry?

TOMBSTONE OF AN OPTIO FROM CHESTER. Can you see his staff of office, sword and writing-tablets? The inscription means: 'To the spirits of the departed Caecilius Aritus of Emerita Augusta (now Merida, in Spain), *optio* of the XX (20th) legion, served 15 years, and lived XXXIIII (34) years. His heirs had this made.'

B

TOMBSTONE OF AN AUXILIARY FROM GLOUCESTER. Can you see his spear, sword and shield, and also the weapon of the Briton being trampled? The inscription reads: 'Rufus Sita, cavalryman of the VI (sixth) Thracian *cohort*, XL (40) years old, XXII (22) years' service, this memorial set up by his heirs.' On discharge an auxiliary became a Roman citizen.

WOUNDED GAUL. Notice the shape of his shield. How would you know from his clothes that he is not a Roman?

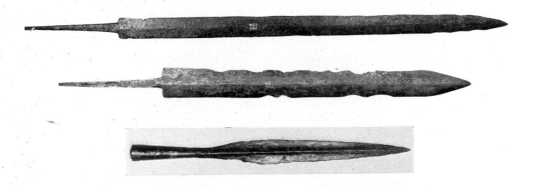

TWO SWORDS AND A SPEARHEAD. Legionaries' weapons were a short double-edged sword for close fighting, and two spears, each seven feet long, for throwing. They also carried tools for making camp, cooking pots and three days' rations.

ARROWHEAD, BOLT FROM BALLISTA (CATAPULT), CALTHROP to be thrown on the ground to hinder cavalry. Auxiliary weapons included slings, and bows and arrows for infantry, and a sword and shield for cavalry (page 23).

LEGIONARY HELMET AND SOLE OF BOOT. Legionaries wore also a tunic and body armour of metal strips. They carried a half-cylindrical shield (pages 23, 25).

FRAGMENTS OF SCALE ARMOUR AND CHAIN MAIL. The clothing and armour of auxiliaries varied according to their place of origin. Some wore a kilt, others wore trousers, some had mail or scale armour, others a leather jerkin. The cavalry carried oval shields (page 23).

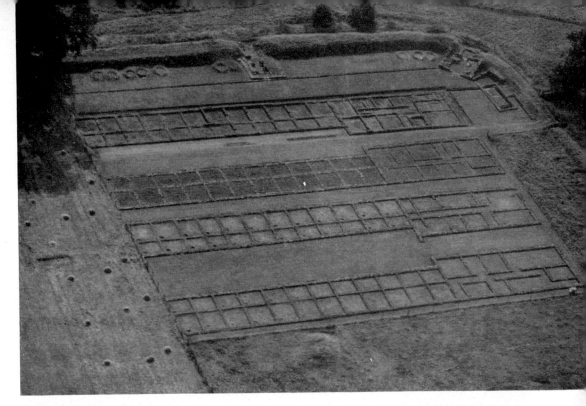

CORNER OF LEGIONARY FORTRESS AT ISCA (CAERLEON). You can see four barrack-blocks, each occupied by a 'century' of 80 men. Each set of two rooms was occupied by 6–8 men, who slept on palliasses in the larger, and stored their equipment in the smaller. The centurion and his staff lived in the large set of rooms at one end. Notice round the wall traces of towers and circular ovens.

GRANARY AT HOUSESTEADS FORT. A year's supply of grain was kept in each Roman fort. Notice the pillars supporting the floor. What do you think was the purpose of this?

WASH PLACES AT HOUSESTEADS, showing remains of washbasins and drains.

THE ROMAN FORT OF HOUSESTEADS FROM THE AIR. This was one of the sixteen forts on Hadrian's Wall, which you can see in the picture. It probably housed a garrison of 500–1,000 auxiliaries. Between the forts were mile-castles and signal-towers to give notice of barbarian attacks. Can you see the remains of the granaries, the four gate-houses, the corner towers, and the civilian buildings outside the walls?

SIGNAL STATION AT SCARBOROUGH FROM THE AIR. Notice the defensive ditch and wall, on the corners of which catapults were mounted. Look for the square base of the tower, from the top of which fire, smoke, and semaphore signals were sent. This was part of the shore defences against Saxon pirates.

THE FORT AT PORTUS ADURNI (PORTCHESTER) FROM THE AIR. This was one of the several shore forts built along the east and south coasts of Britain in the third century A.D. as part of the anti-Saxon defence system. It contained a mixed garrison of soldiers and sailors. Can you see the two main gates, in the east and west walls? The fort was abandoned in the fourth century. The castle and the church were built in the Middle Ages.

THE OUTSIDE WALL OF PORTUS ADURNI (PART OF THE SOUTH SIDE). Although abandoned for some 700 years, these walls served, with some repairs, for the medieval and other fortresses that were to stand on the Roman site.

BUILDING SIEGE PLATFORMS WITH LOGS, shown in sculpture. Behind, legionaries ready for action. On the right auxiliaries are fighting. Pick out stone-slingers in the foreground, Syrian bowmen in coats of mail, and dismounted cavalrymen carrying oval shields.

THE FRONT LINE. CAVALRYMAN HAVING HIS LEG BANDAGED. Behind are the legionary standards and flag. In the foreground Trajan receives a prisoner. Notice the *ballista* on a mule cart: one legionary is loading it, the other is winding up the spring. On the right, notice the half-cylindrical shields of the legionaries and the oval shields of the dismounted cavalry.

ROMAN BRITAIN

- ○ Towns
- Villas
- ---- Main roads
- Legionary forts
- ■ Cohort forts
- + Coastal signal stations

Land over 1000 feet

Swamps and marshes

0   Miles   100

Wall of Antonine

Pons Aelii (Newcastle)

Hadrian's Wall

Segedunum (Wallsend)

Corstopitum (Corbridge)

Luguvallium (Carlisle)

Cataractonium (Catterick)

ISURIUM BRIGANTIUM (Aldborough)

(Lancaster)

EBURACUM (York)

Mamucium (Manchester)

Aquae (Buxton)

Segontium (Caernarvon)

Mona

DEVA (Chester)

LINDUM COLONIA (Lincoln)

Branodunum (Brancaster)

VIROCONIUM CORNOVIORUM @ (Wroxeter)

RATAE CORITANORUM (Leicester)

VENTA ICENORUM (Caistor)

VENTA SILURUM (Caerwent)

Maridunum (Caermarthen)

GLEVUM (Gloucester)

CAMULODUNUM (Colchester)

Othona (Bradwell)

ISCA (Caerleon) (Cardiff)

CORINIUM DOBUNORUM (Cirencester)

VERULAMIUM (St Albans)

LONDINIUM

Regulbium (Reculver)

AQUAE SULIS (Bath)

CALLEVA (Silchester)

DUROVERNUM CANTIACORUM (Canterbury)

Rutupiae (Richborough)

Dubris (Dover)

ISCA DUMNONIORUM (Exeter)

(Ilchester)

VENTA BELGARUM (Winchester)

Lemanis (Lympne)

DURNOVARIA (Dorchester)

REGNUM (Chichester)

Anderida (Pevensey)

Vectis

MAP OF ROMAN BRITAIN SHOWING THE ROAD SYSTEM, built to enable the legions to march quickly to quell rebellions. Trace Watling Street from Dubris through Londinium and Verulamium to Deva, and the Fosse Way from Isca Dumnoniorum, through Aquae Sulis and Corinium, to Lindum. Notice in what parts of the country the forts are distributed, and in what parts the towns and villas.

ROMANS BESIEGING THE ENEMY, shown in sculpture. They are using the 'tortoise'. How is it made? Notice Trajan receiving the heads of enemy chieftains. Legionaries wait on the right. Their spears are missing.

THE ROMANS BEING BESIEGED. Find the bows and arrows and the battering ram that their enemies are using. What are they wearing?

AERIAL VIEW OF LEEMING LANE, CO. DURHAM. It follows the Roman road. Like our modern motor-ways Roman roads were built for high-speed transport of men and equipment. Distances were marked by milestones, and a few of these have been found.

ROMAN ROAD IN YORKSHIRE. These large stones were the foundation for the road. Above these, on the better roads, was a layer of smaller stones, then a mixture of rubble and lime-mortar and, finally, a cambered surface of paving-stones three feet square. At the side were drainage-ditches.

ROMAN TOWNS

There were several different kinds of towns in Roman Britain. Within the native tribal areas, local capitals such as Calleva Atrebatum (Silchester) and many smaller centres, became part of the Imperial administration. Camulodunum (Colchester) and Lindum (Lincoln) were founded to accommodate retired legionaries; Londinium became a centre of trade; Aquae Sulis (Bath) was a spa; and in the north small towns developed from the military villages outside forts.

Most Roman towns are buried under modern towns and are therefore only excavated piece-meal and then covered in. Evidence of plans and buildings is preserved in photographs, taken at the time of excavation, and these are displayed in museums together with utensils, coins, jewellery, mosaic pavements and pottery.

The plans of larger towns are on the grid pattern with streets crossing each other at right-angles. Parts of the defensive wall can be seen at Venta Silurum (Caerwent), and entrance to the town was through fortified gateways in the wall. The centre of the town was the *forum* (page 36) and the basilica (town hall) which was the headquarters of the local government. On the basilica at Viroconium (Wroxeter) is a finely lettered inscription dedicating it to the Emperor Hadrian and thus dating it to A.D. 129–130.

In each town four magistrates (page 30) were elected annually. They became Roman citizens, wore the *toga* and probably celebrated the occasion by paying for games and entertainment at the theatre, or by gifts to the town. They dealt with some lesser court cases, maintained public buildings and collected Imperial taxes. The money from the land tax and the poll tax went to the Imperial treasury and a corn tax was paid to the army. The native tribal area had also to provide materials and labour to keep up the roads and inns and to supply horses for travelling Imperial officials.

Other public buildings, besides the forum and the basilica, included the theatre or amphitheatre (pages 32–4) and temples. An important temple was built at Camulodunum for the worship of the Emperor Claudius; a Mithraic temple (page 38) has been found in Londinium and a possible Christian church at Calleva

Atrebatum (Silchester). Public cemeteries were constructed outside the walls of towns. The bodies were burnt on a bier and then the remains were buried in an urn, usually with food, drink and money for the journey into the next world, together with some small possessions of the dead person.

Another important building was the public baths (page 31), which was also a social centre. Seneca (5 B.C.–A.D. 65), who lived over one in Rome, described the noises that he heard: the slap and hiss of massage; the shouts of the scorers at the ball games; the sounds of people quarrelling; singing and jumping in the plunge-bath; the cries of the cordial-seller, the sausage-man, the puff-pastry-man and of all the eating-house hawkers.

Among the engineering achievements of the Romans were the great aqueducts which supplied water to continental towns, such as Segovia in Spain. In Britain, excavations have shown that water came to Calleva and Venta Silurum (Caerwent) by a gravity supply flowing below ground in timber pipes, and that Lindum (Lincoln) had a public drainage system. The water supply at Viroconium (Wroxeter) was actually tapped for some private houses.

In Calleva most houses consisted of one or more blocks of rooms connected by a veranda along one or both sides. In Venta Silurum and Camulodunum there were also larger, courtyard houses similar to those at Vaizon-la-Romaine (page 29). Several museums display building materials: roofing tiles, fragments of window glass, coloured wall-plaster and mosaic floors. Each house at Calleva had a garden, and seeds have been found showing that the owners grew native plants such as celery, carrot, pea, crabapple, plum, and also introduced species such as grape, fig, and medlar. Some of the larger houses may have been farms. There is also the remains of an iron-smelting furnace, two pottery kilns, a large midden of ox-skulls possibly indicating a leather-tannery, and many shops. The front of each shop had a wooden serving counter, and the back was used for living and working. In these shops were sold some of the luxuries imported from the continent: olive oil, wine, glass, *Samian ware*, engraved semi-precious stones, enamels and bronzes. From shops at Verulamium, where there was a covered walk and bazaar, have come the tools of butcher, knife-maker (page 41), metalworker and carpenter (page 39).

STREET AT VAIZON-LA-ROMAINE, FRANCE. Notice the paving stones and raised curb.

STREET PLAN OF CAIS-TOR-BY-NORWICH FROM THE AIR. This was the capital city of the Iceni, whose Queen was Boudicca (page 3). Notice the chessboard pattern of streets crossing each other at right-angles. The excavations, now covered in, revealed houses and temples.

ROMAN MAGISTRATE. He is wearing a tunic, *toga* and sandals. He holds a *papyrus* roll in his hand, and has a box for others at his feet.

TOMBSTONE TO A MAGISTRATE, P. LICINIUS. It was erected by his two *freedmen* whose portraits are shown. Observe the carvings: *Above*, symbols of magistrate responsible for striking coins—hammer, tongs and coin-die; *left*, symbols of punishment—*fasces* and an axe; *right*, tools of a carpenter—bow-drill, punch, knife, hammer-head and chisel-head.

ROMAN TOWN GATEWAY AT LINDUM (LINCOLN), through which traffic still passes. Notice the round arches, the large one for wheeled vehicles, the smaller one for pedestrians. Parts of the defensive wall and ditch also remain.

PART OF THE PUBLIC BATHS AT CALLEVA ATREBATUM (SILCHESTER), now covered in. The bather went through a series of hot rooms where he sweated and was massaged. Find the pillars on which the floor of the hot room was raised to allow circulation of air, and the cold bath into which the bather plunged finally (compare page 46).

AMPHITHEATRE AT CAERLEON FROM THE AIR. Here were held displays of wild beasts and gladiatorial shows. The banks mark the position of rows of spectators' seats.

MOSAIC SHOWING WINGED CUPIDS DRESSED AS GLADIATORS. Pick out (1) the 'secutor', who wears a helmet, breastplate, greave on his left leg and carries a shield and sword; (2) the 'retiarius', who wears a tunic and carries a sword, trident and net. Each appears in four scenes: two gladiators fighting while an instructor looks on; the 'secutor' defeats the 'retiarius', but the instructor intervenes; the gladiators get ready; the 'retiarius' has fallen and the 'secutor' is about to finish him off.

AMPHITHEATRE AT ARLES FROM THE AIR. In this Roman amphitheatre bull-fights are still held.

CASTOR WARE VASE showing two gladiators. Gladiators were prisoners of war, slaves, criminals or volunteers who were made to fight each other for public amusement at festivals. What weapons and armour has the left-hand gladiator? When the armed one had killed the unarmed one, he was in his turn disarmed and killed by another.

CHARIOT RACE ON A MOSAIC. Such races were held in the Circus Maximus at Rome (page 8) and the chariot might have two horses or four. How many horses has this chariot? How many wheels has it and what has happened to one of them?

THEATRE AT VERULAMIUM. The grassy banks mark the position of rows of seats. In the front rows sat the magistrates and priests. The arena was used for wrestling, bear-baiting and cock-fighting. The pillar marks the front of the stage, which was later extended and used for dancing, singing and pantomime.

THEATRE AT ORANGE showing the façade behind the stage. Shows are still held here in the summer.

THE GREAT BATH AT AQUAE SULIS (BATH). Only the bases of the columns are Roman. In the bath were found many coins and gems thrown in for luck. The water came from a hot spring, and visitors bathed in it as a cure for rheumatic and skin diseases. Near the baths was the Temple of Sul Minerva, the presiding goddess. A bronze head of her was found, and also several inscribed altars, put up as thank-offerings by people who had benefitted from the baths.

PART OF THE FORUM AT RATAE (LEICESTER). The wall may have been part of the basilica (Town Hall). The church behind is medieval.

SOME GODS WORSHIPPED IN ROMAN BRITAIN: JUPITER, the father of the gods. What armour is he wearing? MARS, the god of war. Notice his helmet and plume. LAR, the spirit who looked after the family. A special fire was kept burning on the altar to the Lares, and part of the family meal was sacrificed to them in the flames.

THREE MOTHER GODDESSES.
What are they holding to
symbolise fertility?

MITHRAS SLAYING THE BULL. What is he wearing and how is he slaying the bull? He killed the bull to conquer nature and thereby release the good things of life. Behind him stands his attendant with raised torch signifying day. What does the attendant with lowered torch signify? Mithraism demanded high morals, and a knowledge of the mysteries was gained by passing through ordeals at each stage. Women were excluded and it was practised mainly by the army. There are remains of temples on Hadrian's Wall and in the City of London.

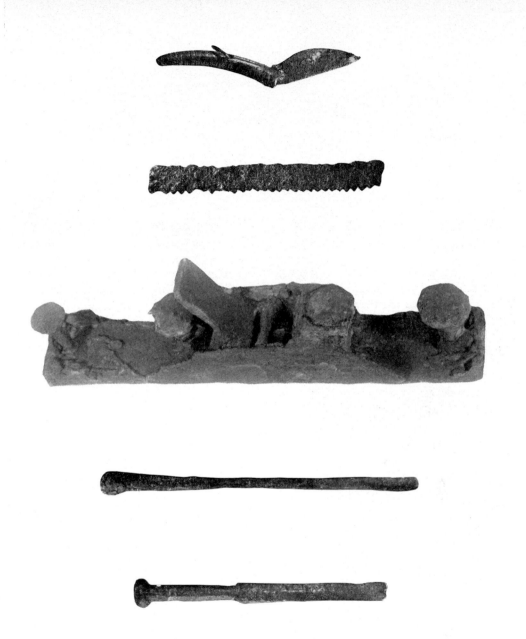

TOOLS OF CARPENTER. Gouge, knife with handle, blade of saw, plane, chisel. Can you identify each of these?

SCHOOLMASTER SITTING BETWEEN TWO PUPILS. Behind one stands the slave who brought him to school and looked after him at home. The children were taught to read, write and count. What kind of books are they using? The famous Roman teacher Quintilian disapproved of flogging, but it was undoubtedly practised. In Italy many boys went on to higher school where they learnt Latin and Greek literature and grammar, and some later went to Athens to study philosophy.

WINE MERCHANT. He is at his counter serving a customer.

CUTLER'S SHOP. What different implements can you see? Notice the dresser on which they are displayed.

BUTCHER'S SHOP. The customer is consulting her shopping list which is written on wax tablets. What is she wearing (page 47), and how is her hair dressed? The butcher is wearing a tunic. What is he doing? The instrument behind him is a steelyard which was used for weighing. Can you see how it worked?

STREET MUSICIANS SHOWN ON A MOSAIC. Find the woman with the pipes; one man with cymbals; another with a tambourine, and a little boy.

THE COUNTRYSIDE

In the countryside many Romano-British people and a few retired Roman soldiers and officials lived on farms, known as villas. The small villas were occupied by small-holders or tenant farmers and the large ones by great landowners. The excavations of some villas, usually where there are mosaics, are kept open, but the majority have been covered in and the evidence preserved in photographs.

In the smaller and earlier villas, such as Ditchley, in Oxfordshire, the main buildings found were the house; the barn for animals, labourers and tools; and the well. Later, a few British villas became very elaborate, like the Roman country estate of Pliny (A.D. 61–113), described in his letters. Bignor, Sussex, is built round two courtyards: in the first, which was surrounded by a corridor, were many rooms with fine mosaics and heating systems (pages 45, 46, 51, 58), the slaves' quarters and a large bath establishment; in the second courtyard was a barn and outbuildings, and round the whole was a wall.

At Lullingstone, in Kent, two portrait busts of eminent Romans, now in the British Museum, have been found. They suggest that in the second century the villa was the home of an important Roman official. Later, these busts were placed in a room converted into a mausoleum, possibly for the worship of ancestors. Finally, in the fourth century, the owners reconstructed some of the rooms as a Christian chapel, in which have been found fragmentary paintings of praying figures and of the Christian monogram (pages 11, 53).

Among the many rooms in a large villa, one of the most important was the dining room. In museums we can find tableware (pages 52–4), cooking utensils (page 55) and occasionally in continental museums, tombstones with sculptured scenes of domestic life (page 50). Among Roman authors, Juvenal describes the 'simple meal' he might have given a guest at his country villa: asparagus and new laid eggs for the hors d'oeuvre, chicken and kid for the main course, and grapes, apples and pears for dessert.

Excavations at *Pompeii* near Naples have revealed a house containing a raised masonry hearth with the bronze cauldrons still standing on their tripods. Most of the cooking was done over a charcoal fire in frying-pans, saucepans and cauldrons on tripods or gridirons (page 55). But joints and porridge were stewed in larger cauldrons slung on chains over wood fires, and a whole animal was roasted on a spit before an open fire. Bread was baked, and smaller joints roasted, in beehive-shaped ovens: charcoal fires were lit inside, raked out when the oven was hot enough, and then the food was put in.

Some Roman recipes have come down to us from Apicius, who lived in Rome in the first century A.D. Most of them show a tendency to disguise the original meat, fish or poultry with elaborate sauces containing many conflicting ingredients. For instance, for pigeons a sauce is made from pepper, borage, parsley, celery-seed, rue, pine-kernels, Jericho dates, honey, vinegar, salt, mustard and a little oil.

Farming was the chief support of the villa. A heavy plough prepared the soil, and crops were harvested with scythes and sickles (page 57). Some villas contain traces of a specially prepared hard floor where grain was threshed by a heavy sledge. In smaller villas the grain was stored in basket-lined pits, after being dried in special ovens. Lullingstone had a large barn raised on pillars to enable air to circulate beneath and thus assist in drying the corn above. Corn was grown to feed both natives and the army, but later the Imperial government also encouraged sheep and cattle farming for woollen cloth and leather.

Roman agriculture in all its aspects, from crops and stock to bees and fruit, is brought alive for us by the poet *Virgil* in his *Georgics*. 'Plough in the warm months in your shirt-sleeves', he says; and he also describes winter work: 'acorns to gather, and berries off the bay tree, and olives and blood-red myrtle; now you can lay your traps for the crane, your nets for the stag'.

In the countryside there were also shrines, though little of them remains above ground. Some of these, such as Gosbecks near Camulodunum, were centres of local trade. Others, such as the healing shrine of the god Nodens at Lydney, in Gloucestershire, possessed many bedrooms and a bath-house for pilgrims. Tombs were also built in the countryside, and the six conical hills on Roman Ermine Street at Stevenage, Hertfordshire, are a well-known example.

THE NORTH WING OF CHEDWORTH VILLA. This shows the walls of a series of rooms, possibly workshops and outbuildings. The villa was built round three sides of a square courtyard. Notice the bases of the columns which formed a colonnade.

BATHING ESTABLISHMENT. Part of the hot room and of the sweating room at Chedworth. There was a furnace outside, fuelled by charcoal, and heat flowed under the floors and up flues in the walls. Find the pillars supporting the floor and the box flues at the base of the far wall. Compare this with the public baths at Calleva Atrebatum, shown on page 31.

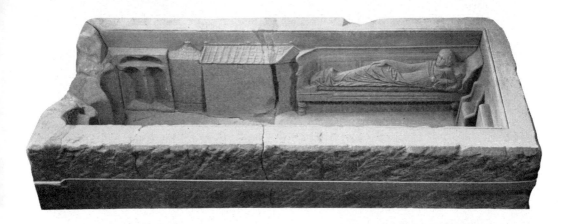

BUILDINGS AND FURNITURE: TWO VIEWS OF A TOMB. Find the following: villa with bath-house attached; sofa; cupboard with panelled doors; shelves with toilet vessels; three-legged table; and bench with jugs. There was also gold jewellery and a silver mirror. The lady is wearing a stole, and over it a mantle. Can you see her brooch?

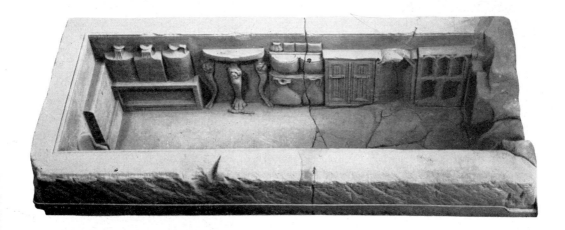

TOMBSTONE OF REGINA. The inscription says that she was a freed slavewomen of the tribe of Catuvellauni (Hertfordshire), the wife of Barates, a Palmyrene (Syrian), and that she was XXX (30) years old. Notice her casket with its keyhole, and her workbasket. What is she wearing?

TOMBSTONE OF JULIA VELVA. The inscription says that she was L (50) years old and that her heir erected the tomb on behalf of himself and his family. Can you identify Julia, her heir, her daughter and her granddaughter? Notice the three-legged table on which was set food for the feast of the dead, and the large mattress on which Julia lies.

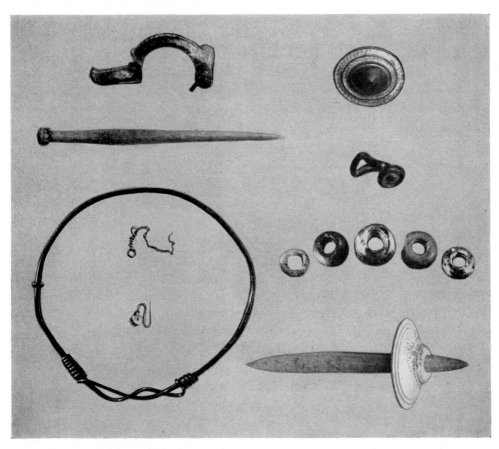

ORNAMENTS. Find the following: cross-bar brooch, round bronze brooch, bone hair-pin, button, bracelet, earrings, beads. The spindle and whorl were used for *spinning*.

CARNELIAN FROM A FINGER-RING. Can you see the ship, and the lighthouse with smoke coming from the top?

MEAL, SHOWN ON TOMBSTONE. *Left to right*: slaves serving wine, the family dining, slaves cooking. Can you distinguish the two men reclining and the two women sitting in chairs? The cooking is being done on a raised masonry hearth. The food was eaten off plates with fingers, spoons and knives.

TOMBSTONE SHOWING AN OLD WOMAN HAVING HER HAIR DRESSED BY FOUR MAIDS. What is the maid holding in front of her? What is the chair made of?

MOSAIC SHOWING THE MYTHICAL HERO BELLEROPHON riding Pegasus and killing the monster called the chimaera. Notice the wings on Pegasus, the sea creatures and the faces of the seasons. How is the chimaera being killed?

MOSAIC SHOWING THE GOD JUPITER, disguised as a bull, carrying off Europa across the sea. One Cupid seems to be encouraging the bull. What is the other doing?

SILVER TABLEWARE. Part of a magnificent set, made abroad but discovered in a Suffolk field where its owners probably buried it after the fall of Rome. BOWL AND COVER. Find the half-animal, half-human figure. GOBLET. BOWL. How many animals can you recognize?

SILVER TABLEWARE. Part of the same set as shown on page 52. DISH. The large figures show a scene of feasting. Find goat-footed Pan with his reed-pipes; Bacchus with his foot on a panther; Hercules drunk; the dancing girls; the man playing the double-pipes. LADLE. Notice the dolphin handle. SPOON. Look for the Christian monogram ☧.

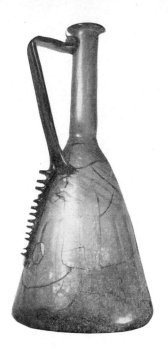

TWO GLASS WINE FLASKS. Glass flasks, bowls and plates were increasingly imported into Britain from the Rhineland from the end of the third century A.D.

FINE POTTERY. *Left to right*: *Samian* dish, bone spoon, *Castor* beaker, Samian bowl, bronze spoon, Samian drinking cup, Samian plate.

KITCHEN POTTERY. *Above, left to right*: skillet, amphora for storing wine or oil, cooking pot. The skillet and the cooking pot are blackened by fire. What would have been cooked in them? *Below, left to right*: mortar with grit in the bottom for grinding up food, cheese press with holes in the bottom, flask for serving wine or water, colander for straining vegetables.

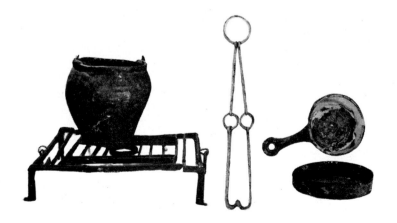

KITCHEN UTENSILS Gridiron with cauldron. Pothook (for suspending large cauldrons). Patera or saucepan. Frying-pan. What are these utensils used for?

POTTERY LAMP. What is the picture? Olive oil was put into the lamp through the central hole, and a wick burnt in the nozzle.

WRITING MATERIALS. Wooden tablets which were coated with wax on which the letters were scratched with a stilus (*left*). An inkpot and a bronze pen for writing on either *papyrus* or on *vellum*. The ink was probably made from lamp-black.

AGRICULTURAL TOOLS. Shears for shearing sheep. Scythe blade which would have been attached to a long handle. Axe with a modern handle. Padlock and five ankle shackles perhaps used for slaves. Coulter for a plough: it is placed in front of the share and cuts the soil so that the share can pass more easily. Can you tell which of the tools is which?

HAND QUERN. Corn is put in through the hole in the top stone, the handle is turned to grind the top stone on the bottom, and the flour comes out between the two.

MOSAIC. TWO SCENES FROM VIRGIL'S STORY OF DIDO AND AENEAS. (1) The arrival of Aeneas' fleet. A jewelled collar is being handed ashore as a present for Dido. Notice the beaked ships with small sails and oars. (2) *Left to right*: Aeneas' son, Aeneas and Dido out hunting. Notice their striped cloaks. Dido later killed herself because Aeneas had to leave her to continue his mission to found Rome. (In places the mosaic has been damaged.)

Glossary

Ballista A large catapult, used in seige-warfare, for shooting stones or beams.

Caesar, Gaius Julius (102–44 B.C.) Great soldier and statesman, assassinated by those who feared he might make himself king. His *Commentaries* describe his campaigns in Gaul and his two expeditions to Britain.

Castor ware Black pottery, made at Castor, Northamptonshire.

Christendom The community of all people professing Christianity.

Cohort An army unit of six centuries of 80 men each. Ten cohorts made up a legion.

Colonia A city or a settlement occupied by retired Roman soldiers.

Decimate To punish a division of soldiers by executing one man in ten (chosen by lot).

Druids Priests of a British religion showing fanatical opposition to the Romans. They worshipped the mistletoe and the oak and also practised human sacrifice.

Fasces The bundle of rods carried in public in front of high magistrates. An axe was inserted into the bundle and signified the power of punishment or death. The fasces were, recently, the symbol of the Italian fascists, led by Mussolini.

Forum The market place in a town where people met for business. It contained trading halls, law courts, baths and shops.

Freedman Roman slaves were sometimes freed by their masters, and their sons were then free-born men.

Gaul (Latin *Gallia*) A province of the Roman Empire, corresponding to modern France and parts of Belgium and Germany.

Josephus (A.D. 38–after 100) A Jewish general and eye-witness of Vespasian's destruction of Jerusalem in A.D. 70, which he describes in his *Jewish War*.

Middle Ages The period of time between the end of the Roman Empire (A.D. 410) and the Renaissance (about the fifteenth century).

Optio The second-in-command in a century to the centurion, who often chose his own optio. Compare our word 'optional'.

Papyrus Paper made from the stem of a water plant called papyrus. A papyrus book was in the form of a roll.

Pompeii An Italian town buried by the eruption of Vesuvius in A.D. 79. Excavations have revealed many buildings, and their contents, which give a very good picture of town life.

Samian ware Red-glazed pottery, often ornamented with reliefs, imported into Britain from Gaul.

Senate During the Empire, a council, consisting of former high magistrates, who advised the Emperor.

Spinning Combed wool was placed on a stick and held under the left arm. A thread was drawn out and attached to the spindle which was spun with the right hand. The circular whorl helped to keep the spindle spinning.

Tacitus (about A.D. 55–120) Famous for his history of the early Emperors, his account of the German tribes and his biography of Agricola.

Toga Semicircular woollen garment worn draped over the left shoulder. The toga of citizens was white, those of Emperor, magistrates and priests had a purple border.

Trophy Pile of captured armour and weapons set up by the victors.

Vellum Fine sheet of the skin of calf, lamb or kid. In the fourth century A.D. books of vellum sheets began to take the place of the papyrus roll.

Virgil (70–19 B.C.) Famous Roman poet. He wrote the *Eclogues*, idyllic stories about shepherds, the *Georgics*, describing agricultural work, and the *Aeneid*, the story of the travels of Aeneas of Troy and of his supposed foundation of Rome.

Some Sources to Consult

Books

Roman Britain, and *Ancient Rome*.
Then and There Series (Longmans).
Everyday things in Roman Britain.
Marjorie and C. H. B. Quennell.
Daily life in Ancient Rome.
Jérôme Carcopino (Penguin).
The Roman Commonwealth. R. W. Moore.
The Romans in Britain, Inscriptions.
Translated A. R. Burn.
Roman Britain. R. Sellman.
Roman Panorama. H. Grose-Hodge.
Roman history from coins. M. Grant.
The Roman Army. G. Webster.
(Grosvenor Museum, Chester.)

Latin Authors in English Translation

The first five authors are in Penguin editions.
Julius Caesar, *The Conquest of Gaul*.
Plutarch, *The Fall of the Roman Republic*.
Tacitus, *Annals of Imperial Rome*.
Tacitus, *Agricola*.
Josephus, *The Jewish War*.
Virgil, *The Georgics*, trans. C. Day Lewis.

Museums with Roman Collections

In London:
    The British Museum.
    The London Museum.
    The Guildhall Museum.

The Castle Museum, Colchester.
The Yorkshire Museum, York.
The Silchester Collection, Reading Museum
The Verulamium Museum, St. Albans.
The Grosvenor Museum, Chester.

Roman Sites

Hadrian's Wall and Housesteads Fort, Northumberland.
Richborough Castle, Kent.
Bignor Roman villa, Sussex.
Caerleon, South Wales.

There are many other museum collections and sites which are referred to in the Index.

Acknowledgements

We are grateful to the following for their kind assistance in providing photographs:

Pages 5, 6 (middle), *7* (left), *8, 9, 11* (bottom), *16* (bottom), *18* (top), *30* (bottom), *34, 37* (top), *52* and *53* The British Museum: *Page 58,* Somerset County Museum, Taunton: *Pages 6* (top), *7* (right), *11* (bottom), *15* (left) and *33* (bottom) Colchester Museum: *Page 10* Alinari: *Pages 12* (top), *18* (bottom left), *38* and *56* London Museum: *Page 12* Ashmolean Museum: *Pages 2, 15* (right), *23, 25* Grosvenor Museum, Chester: *Page 16* (top) City Museum, Gloucester: *Pages 17* and *18* (bottom right) National Museum of Antiquities, Edinburgh: *Pages 19, 32* (top) and *35* (top) Photoflight: *Pages 20, 22* (bottom) and *51* Ministry of Works: *Pages 21, 22* (top), *26* (top) and *29* (bottom) The Curator in Aerial Photography, Cambridge University: *Page 24* Based on a map in *Roman Britain* by R. R. Sellman (Methuen): *Pages 6* (bottom), *26* (bottom) and *48* (bottom) York Museum: *Pages 29* (top), *33* (top) and *35* (bottom) Caisse Nationale Des Monuments Historiques: *Page 30* (top) Dr. Vagn Poulsen, Glyptotheque, Carlsberg: *Page 31* (top) Record and General Photographs, Lincoln: *Pages 31* (bottom), *39, 49* (top) and *55* (bottom) Reading Museum: *Page 32* (bottom) Captain H. Tupper: *Page 36* (top) Spa Department, Bath Corporation: *Page 32* (bottom) Leicester Museum: *Page 37* (bottom) Corinium Museum: *Pages 40* (top), *41* (bottom) and *50* Landesmuseum, Trier: *Page 40* (bottom) Dijon Museum: *Page 41* (top) Vatican Museum: *Page 42* Museo Nationale, Naples: *Pages 45* and *46* A. F. Kersting: *Page 47* Leiden Museum: *Page 48* (top) South Shields Public Libraries and Museums Committee: *Page 49* (bottom and top) Norwich Museum: *Page 54* (top) Royal Museum, Canterbury: *Pages 54* (bottom) and *55* (top) J. H. Brown: *Page 57* (top) Department of Archaeology and Ethnology, Cambridge University: *Page 57* (bottom) Sussex Archaeological Society.

Index and List of Sources

References in text thus, 6. References to pictures thus, **6**.

LONGMANS, GREEN AND CO LTD
6 & 7 CLIFFORD STREET, LONDON W1
605–611 LONSDALE STREET, MELBOURNE C1
443 LOCKHART ROAD, HONG KONG
ACCRA, AUCKLAND, IBADAN
KINGSTON (JAMAICA), KUALA LUMPUR
LAHORE, NAIROBI, SALISBURY (RHODESIA)
LONGMANS SOUTHERN AFRICA (PTY) LTD
THIBAULT HOUSE, THIBAULT SQUARE, CAPE TOWN

LONGMANS, GREEN AND CO INC
119 WEST 40TH STREET, NEW YORK 18

LONGMANS, GREEN AND CO
137 BOND STREET, TORONTO 2

ORIENT LONGMANS PRIVATE LTD
CALCUTTA, BOMBAY, MADRAS
DELHI, HYDERABAD, DACCA

© ISLAY DONCASTER 1961
First Edition 1961
Printed in Great Britain by
SPOTTISWOODE, BALLANTYNE & CO LTD
LONDON & COLCHESTER